GREAT WAYS WITH POTATOES

CONTENTS

GREAT WAYS WITH POTATOES

The potato is one of our most valuable basic foods. This mainstay has inspired many irresistible dishes—both simple and elegant, hearty and light—from around the world.

NORTHERN & EASTERN EUROPE

LATIN AMERICA

Rugged, green Western South America is the birthplace of the potato. "Inca Gold," as the vegetable is sometimes affectionately known, has been cultivated in the Andes for millennia. Now as then, each potato must be picked by hand—the remote Highlands are inaccessible to heavy machinery. But the rewards of such labor are great, and the harvest is enjoyed in various ways. Panfried until golden, pureed until smooth, or spiced with lively chiles, the potato is always appealing.

When first introduced to Europe, the potato was mistrusted as a vegetable not mentioned in the Bible, but parts of Europe soon learned to embrace it. Later, legend has it, Prussia's Frederick the Great

THE MIDDLE EAST

The Israeli kitchen is known for its creative and delectable combinations of Eastern European and Middle Eastern cooking traditions. Potato dishes from this region—seasoned with cumin, thyme, and other fragrant spices and fresh herbs—deliciously reflect these dual influences.

ASIA

4

NORTH AMERICA & AUSTRALIA

Baked or stuffed, mashed or fried—the potato is enjoyed in all possible ways in the United States and Australia. Wonderful sauces and spicy combinations crown the wholesome root vegetable, which always makes a great side or main dish.

THE MEDITERRANEAN

Savory tortillas, frittatas, and hearty gnocchi are among the warming Mediterranean specialties made with the potato. Cooks from this part of the world have come up with many imaginative and colorful preparations for the popular food, often pairing it with another vegetable and a variety of flavor-packed seasonings, such as fresh and dried herbs, pungent garlic, and zesty lemon.

helped to make the potato one of Europe's most important staples. Since then, the region has produced some of the world's finest potato dishes, among them croquettes, dumplings, and various gratins.

The potato is not frequently seen on the table in this region. But when it does appear, it's usually prepared with traditional ingredients—like curry and coconut—and featured in luscious, aromatic dishes.

PARSLIED POTATOES

ENGLAND

This sumptuous side dish hails from England, where it's often paired with fish or roasted chicken. Worcestershire sauce adds a piquant note to the irresistibly creamy sauce.

INGREDIENTS
(Serves 4)

- 2 pounds baking potatoes
- 1 cup Italian parsley leaves
- 1 medium onion
- 2 tablespoons butter
- 2 tablespoons all-purpose flour
- 1 cup heavy cream
- ½ cup vegetable broth
- ½ cup milk
- salt and pepper
- ½ teaspoon Worcestershire sauce

INGREDIENT TIP

Flat-leaf Italian parsley is more flavorful than the curly variety—but the choice is yours. If you prefer, you can use ¼ cup chopped dill instead—dilled potatoes taste particularly good with fish.

1 Peel the potatoes and slice ¼-inch thick. Bring a large saucepan of lightly salted water to a boil. Add the potatoes and simmer for 5 minutes, until almost tender. Drain in a colander.

Step 1

2 Meanwhile, finely chop the parsley. Peel and dice the onion. Melt the butter in a deep skillet over medium-low heat. Add the onion; cook until tender, about 5 minutes. Add the flour and stir for 2 minutes. Whisk in the cream, broth, and milk. Continue to cook until hot and thick, about 5 minutes.

Step 2

3 Add the partially cooked potatoes and half of the parsley to the cream sauce. Stir in ¾ teaspoon salt, ½ teaspoon pepper, and the Worcestershire sauce.

4 Simmer the potatoes over medium-low heat for about 7 minutes, until meltingly tender. Sprinkle with the remaining parsley and serve hot or warm.

Step 4

Preparation: 10 minutes
Cooking: 30 minutes
Per serving: 448 cal; 7 g pro;
29 g fat; 42 g carb.

TYPICALLY ENGLISH

If England had a national condiment, it would surely be Worcestershire sauce. Vinegar, molasses, sugar, garlic, anchovies, tamarind, shallots, and a mixture of spices all add to its distinctive flavor. The exact recipe has been a well-kept secret for over 150 years.

COOKING TIP

The basis of this potato dish is béchamel—a French white sauce made by stirring milk into a mixture of butter and flour. It is important to simmer the sauce for at least 5 minutes (preferably 10 minutes) to ensure that the taste of the flour disappears.

SERVING TIPS

Offer these potatoes as a side dish with a centerpiece of juicy, pink roast beef.

 Enjoy a glass of Cabernet Sauvignon, a pint of English Ale, or some cider with this dish.

IRELAND

The Irish version of mashed potatoes, colcannon is made with savoy cabbage, scallions, and nutmeg for a hint of spice. It's just the thing to warm you up on a really cold day.

INGREDIENTS
(Serves 4)

- 2 pounds baking potatoes
- ½ pound savoy cabbage (about ¼ of a large head)
- 1 bunch of scallions
- 4 tablespoons butter
- 1 cup milk
- salt and pepper
- pinch of nutmeg

IN ADDITION

- 2 tablespoons parsley for garnish

INGREDIENT TIP

Ranging in color from pale to dark green, savoy cabbage is particularly good for cooking. Watch for crisp-looking leaves, and choose a head that feels heavy for its size.

1 Peel the potatoes and cut into 1-inch chunks. Place in a medium saucepan with water to cover. Bring to a simmer; cook gently until tender, about 20 minutes.

2 Meanwhile, core the cabbage and thinly slice into shreds with a large, sharp knife. Place in a saucepan with water to cover. Simmer until wilted, about 5 minutes. Drain and set aside.

3 Trim and thinly slice the scallions. Melt the butter in the same saucepan used for the cabbage. Add the scallions and cook, stirring, for 2 minutes. Return the cabbage to the pan, add the milk, and bring to a simmer over medium heat. Remove from heat.

4 Drain the potatoes well in a colander. Place in a large bowl and mash. Stir in the warm cabbage mixture, ½ teaspoon salt, ¼ teaspoon pepper, and the nutmeg. Sprinkle the parsley on top and serve.

Step 2

Step 3

Step 4

Preparation: 25 minutes
Cooking: 20 minutes
Per serving: 299 cal; 7 g pro; 14 g fat; 39 g carb.

TYPICALLY IRISH

The potato has been cultivated and relished in Ireland since the late 16th century. It was valued immediately as a hearty crop that thrived even in poor soils and required little equipment for harvesting.

COOKING TIP

If you want the cabbage tender-crisp, skip the preboil step (Step 2). Just sauté the raw chopped leaves in the butter (Step 3). You'll particularly enjoy the results when you use very fresh young cabbage.

SERVING TIPS

Smoked bacon, ham, and sausages are delicious with these savory mashed potatoes.

 Serve cold beer—perhaps Guinness or another Irish brew—with your meal.

$\mathscr{S}$ALMON-POTATO SALAD

Potatoes, cured salmon, and sugar snap peas are an unbeatable combination. A light, creamy dill mayonnaise rounds out this main-dish salad wonderfully.

INGREDIENTS
(Serves 4)

- 1½ pounds small white potatoes
- ¼ pound snow peas
- ¼ pound gravlax or lox

FOR THE MAYONNAISE

- 1 egg yolk, at room temperature
- 1 tablespoon flour
- 1 tablespoon cider vinegar
- 1 tablespoon lemon juice
- 1 tablespoon plus ½ cup canola oil
- salt and pepper
- ½ teaspoon dry mustard
- ¼ cup chopped fresh dill plus sprigs for garnish
- cracked black pepper

INGREDIENT TIP

You can also use flaked fresh poached salmon—warm or chilled—in this salad.

1 Peel the potatoes. Cook in salted water for 20–25 minutes, until fork-tender. Drain, let cool, then slice ¼ inch thick. Meanwhile, trim the snow peas. Cook in a small pot of simmering water for 2 minutes. Drain and rinse with cold water.

2 Place the egg yolk in a medium bowl; beat with an electric mixer until light and fluffy. Set aside. In a small saucepan, whisk together the flour, vinegar, lemon juice, 1 tablespoon of the oil and ½ cup water. Bring to a boil, stirring constantly. Continue to cook for 3 minutes, until thickened slightly.

3 Gradually beat the hot mixture into the yolks. Let cool to room temperature, then beat in the remaining ½ cup oil, pouring in a fine stream. Stir in ¾ teaspoon salt, ¼ teaspoon pepper, the mustard and dill.

4 Slice the salmon. Arrange potatoes, peas and salmon on individual plates. Drizzle the mayonnaise on top. Garnish the salads with dill sprigs and cracked pepper.

Step 1

Step 3

Step 4

Preparation: 45 minutes
Cooking: 25 minutes
Per serving: 442 cal; 10 g pro; 33 g fat; 27 g carb.

TYPICALLY SWEDISH

Gravlax, a salt-and-sugar-cured salmon, was originally preserved for times of need. Now a famous Scandinavian specialty, gravlax is served at luxury hotels and elegant restaurants, as well as simpler eateries and rustic country inns.

COOKING TIPS

• You'll have the best results making the mayonnaise if all of the ingredients are at room temperature.

• It's important to add only a little oil at a time—stir carefully between additions until the oil is completely incorporated into the yolk.

SERVING TIPS

An apple-almond cake served with vanilla sauce is a great follow-up to this dish.

A glass of ice-cold aquavit makes a perfect refreshment either before or after the meal.

SERVING TIPS With these flavorful, bite-size appetizers, offer dark crispbread and butter.

 This dish is best served with a Danish beer, ice-cold clear schnapps, or nonalcoholic punch.

𝒫OTATO CANAPÉS

DENMARK

INGREDIENTS
(Serves 4)

- 1 pound fingerling or small white new potatoes
- 1 tablespoon fresh dill sprigs, plus more for garnish
- ½ cup sour cream
- 2 tablespoons mayonnaise
- 1 teaspoon lemon juice
- salt and white pepper
- 4 ounces sliced smoked salmon or gravlax
- 4 ounces smoked whitefish
- lettuce leaves for garnish
- 2 tablespoons caviar

INGREDIENT TIP

Salmon roe and lumpfish roe offer good value for your money as an alternative to genuine Russian caviar.

These tasty morsels were inspired by "smørrebrød," the Danish open-faced sandwiches. Instead of bread, potato slices create a tender base for small pieces of fish and delicious dill cream.

1 Scrub the potatoes and place in a medium saucepan with water to cover. Lightly salt the water and bring to a boil. Reduce the heat and simmer until the potatoes are fork-tender, about 30 minutes. Drain and let cool slightly, then trim and cut into 24 slices about ½ inch thick.

2 Finely chop the dill. Place in a bowl with the sour cream, mayonnaise, lemon juice, ¼ teaspoon salt, and ⅛ teaspoon white pepper. Stir well to blend.

3 Cut portions of fish into 24 (total) pieces. Wash the lettuce and arrange on a serving platter.

4 Place a piece of smoked fish and some of the dilled sour cream neatly on each of the potato slices. Transfer the canapés carefully to the serving platter. Garnish each with some of the caviar and a dill sprig.

Step 1

Step 3

Step 4

Preparation: 20 minutes
Cooking: 30 minutes
Per serving: 287 cal; 17 g pro; 15 g fat; 22 g carb.

TYPICALLY DANISH

Denmark's picturesque Baltic Sea islands—particularly Bornholm—are considered by many to be the birthplace of smoked herring.

CRISP POTATO PANCAKES

GERMANY

These potato pancakes are a real treat when they're freshly made—golden and crunchy on the outside, soft on the inside. They're served here with a delicious, fruity, tart applesauce.

INGREDIENTS
(Serves 4)

FOR THE APPLESAUCE
- 1½ pounds tart apples
- ½ cup apple juice
- 2 tablespoons lemon juice
- 1 tablespoon sugar

FOR THE PANCAKES
- 2 pounds all-purpose potatoes
- 1 medium onion
- ½ cup sour cream
- ½ cup plain bread crumbs
- 3 large eggs, lightly beaten
- salt and pepper

IN ADDITION
- ½ cup vegetable oil, for frying

INGREDIENT TIP

The sauce tastes best when made with tart apples, such as Granny Smith, Cortland, Gravenstein, or Greening.

1 Peel, quarter, and core the apples, then thinly slice them. Place in a saucepan with the apple juice, lemon juice, and sugar. Simmer until tender, about 10 minutes.

Step 1

2 Peel then coarsely grate the potatoes. Place in a large bowl of cold water and let rest for several minutes. With your hands, transfer the shreds of potato to a colander to drain, then spread out on a kitchen towel. Cover with a second towel, roll up, and squeeze to remove excess moisture. Place the potato in a large bowl.

Step 2

3 Peel and finely chop the onion. Add to the potatoes with the sour cream, bread crumbs, and eggs. Add 1 teaspoon salt and ½ teaspoon pepper and mix well.

4 Heat ¼ cup of the oil in a nonstick skillet over medium-high heat. Cook the pancakes in batches, adding ¼ cup of the potato mixture for each and flattening with a spatula, until golden brown, about 4 minutes. (Add the remaining ¼ cup oil as necessary.) Serve with the applesauce.

Step 4

Preparation: 30 minutes
Cooking: 20 minutes
Per serving: 592 cal; 12 g pro; 29 g fat; 75 g carb.

TYPICALLY GERMAN

The much-loved potato pancake is standard mealtime fare in many parts of Germany. It's a particular favorite in the Rhine River Valley, where it often graces the dinner menu during important holidays.

COOKING TIP

To make the pancakes delectably crisp, use plenty of hot oil. Flip them only when the first side has turned golden. Let the finished pancakes drain briefly in a single layer on paper towels.

SERVING TIPS

Any tangy fruit sauce is nice—try cranberry. Or serve with berry jams or cinnamon-sugar.

 Offer apple juice or cider for your guests to drink with this dish.

SUGARED POTATO DUMPLINGS

GERMANY

A favorite German dessert, these golden dumplings make a luscious endnote to brunch—or a sweet bite anytime. Served with whipped cream and cinnamon-sugar, they're irresistible.

INGREDIENTS
(Serves 6)

- 1 pound small baking potatoes
- 1 lemon
- ½ cup sour cream
- 2 tablespoons flour
- 2 tablespoons sugar
- 2 large eggs, beaten
- ⅛ teaspoon baking powder
- salt
- ¼ cup raisins

IN ADDITION
- ½ cup vegetable oil for frying
- 1 cup heavy cream
- cinnamon-sugar

INGREDIENT TIP

A flavorless vegetable oil is desirable for this dish. Try canola, which is the lowest in saturated fat of all the oils.

1 Place the unpeeled potatoes in a medium saucepan with water to cover. Bring to a boil, reduce the heat, and simmer until fork-tender, about 30 minutes. Drain, let cool slightly, then peel the potatoes and press through a ricer into a large bowl.

Step 1

2 Finely grate 2 teaspoons of peel from the lemon. Add to the potato with the sour cream, flour, sugar, eggs, baking powder, and ½ teaspoon salt. Mix well; stir in the raisins. Cover and let stand for 30 minutes.

3 Using 2 soup spoons, make oval dumplings with the potato mixture. Place on a well-floured board and flatten each slightly with floured hands.

Step 3

4 Heat the oil in a large skillet over medium-high heat. In batches, add the dumplings to the pan without crowding; fry on both sides until golden, about 3 minutes.

5 Drain on paper towels and keep warm. Whip the cream until soft. Sprinkle the dumplings with cinnamon-sugar and serve immediately with the cream.

Step 4

Preparation: 30 minutes
Cooking: 40 minutes
Standing: 30 minutes
Per Portion: 435 cal; 6 g pro; 32 g fat; 32 g carb.

TYPICALLY GERMAN
Germany is a prolific producer of potatoes. In some regions they are still harvested by hand. King Frederic II was one of the first European rulers to cultivate the popular root vegetable.

COOKING TIP

Try this variation: Omit the sugar and raisins. Add chopped herbs, salt, and pepper, and sprinkle with Parmesan cheese to transform the dumplings into a sophisticated savory side dish.

SERVING TIPS

Offer this dessert with a warm but not overly sweet compote made of dried fruits.

 Coffee, tea, or fruit juice will go quite nicely with these scrumptious treats.

POTATO-STUFFED CABBAGE

POLAND

Here's a special side dish from Poland—fresh red cabbage filled with a creamy potato-and-onion mixture. It's beautiful to look at, as well as tasty to eat.

INGREDIENTS
(Serves 4)

- 1½ pounds baking potatoes
- 1 medium onion
- 3 tablespoons vegetable oil
- 2 egg yolks
- salt and white pepper
- ¼ teaspoon paprika
- pinch of cayenne pepper
- 8 large or 16 small red cabbage leaves
- ⅔ cup chicken broth
- chopped parsley

INGREDIENT TIP

Traditionally, these rolls are cooked with duck or goose fat, which is rendered when a bird is roasted. If you prefer, you can fry the rolls in lard or butter.

1 In a medium saucepan, cover the unpeeled potatoes with salted water. Cook until fork-tender, 35–40 minutes.

2 Meanwhile, peel and chop the onion. In a small skillet, heat 1 tablespoon oil over medium heat and sauté the onion until translucent, about 3 minutes.

3 Peel the potatoes and press through a ricer into a bowl. Add the onion, egg yolks, 1 teaspoon salt, ½ teaspoon white pepper, the paprika, and cayenne. Mix well.

4 Cut the core from the cabbage leaves. In a large saucepan of simmering water, cook the leaves for 5 minutes, until pliable. Drain and pat dry with paper towels.

5 Shape the potato mixture into 8 or 16 equal-size croquettes. Roll up each in a cabbage leaf. Heat the remaining oil in a large skillet over medium heat and fry the rolls, seam-side down, for 5 minutes.

6 Add the broth, cover, and simmer the rolls, turning them occasionally, until heated through, about 10 minutes. Place on serving dishes and sprinkle with the parsley.

Step 4

Step 5

Step 6

Preparation: 20 minutes
Cooking: 55 minutes
Per serving: 304 cal; 7 g pro; 14 g fat; 41 g carb.

TYPICALLY POLISH

When fresh locally grown produce becomes scarce in Poland in the winter, cooks traditionally turn to an abundant reserve of pickled cabbage. Over the years, the Polish people have come up with many creative uses for the economical vegetable.

COOKING TIP

If you have difficulty removing the cabbage leaves from the head, put the cabbage in boiling water for a few minutes first, then remove the leaves and cook them individually as described in Step 4.

SERVING TIPS

Try this side dish with fried sausage and caramelized onions. It's also delicious with roast duck.

Finish your meal as the Polish do—have a small glass of ice-cold vodka.

SERVING TIPS A fresh green salad or buttered
cooked carrots goes very nicely alongside the ravioli.

 Enjoy this sumptuous meal with a glass of white
wine, such as a Rhine Riesling.

20

ℋERBED POTATO POCKETS

AUSTRIA

It's easy to make and fill these delicate, savory pouches of pasta. Creamy ricotta cheese and a variety of your favorite fresh herbs combine with potatoes to make a delectable filling.

INGREDIENTS
(Serves 4)

- 1⅓ cups unbleached flour
- 3 large eggs, beaten
- salt and pepper
- 1 large baking potato, peeled and quartered
- ⅓ cup ricotta cheese
- 1 tablespoon sour cream or milk
- 1 tablespoon minced fresh herbs, such as chives, chervil, parsley, and mint
- ⅛ teaspoon nutmeg

IN ADDITION

- 5 bacon strips
- 3 tablespoons butter
- 1 tablespoon minced chives

INGREDIENT TIP

All-purpose flour makes a delicious pasta dough here. If you prefer, use whole-wheat pastry flour, which you'll find at most health-food stores.

1 In a bowl, stir together the flour, eggs, ½ teaspoon salt, and 1 tablespoon water. Knead on a floured board until smooth, about 5 minutes. Let stand for 30 minutes.

2 Meanwhile, place the potato in a medium saucepan with water to cover. Bring to a simmer; cook until tender, about 20 minutes. Drain and mash in a bowl. Stir in the ricotta, sour cream, herbs, ¼ teaspoon salt, ⅛ teaspoon pepper, and the nutmeg.

3 Bring a large pot of salted water to a boil. Meanwhile, lightly flour the board. Roll out the dough to an 18-inch square, about ⅛ inch thick. With a 3-inch biscuit cutter, cut out about 2 dozen circles.

4 Brush the edges of each circle with water and place a rounded teaspoon of filling in the center. Fold in half, sealing well by pressing with your fingers. Cook in the boiling water until tender, 12–15 minutes.

5 Finely chop the bacon. Fry in the butter in a skillet over medium heat until crisp. Add the pockets and turn to coat in the butter. Sprinkle with chives and serve hot.

Step 2

Step 4

Step 5

Preparation: 30 minutes
Standing: 30 minutes
Cooking: 20 minutes
Per serving: 519 cal; 15 g pro; 33 g fat; 41 g carb.

TYPICALLY AUSTRIAN
The mountainous southernmost region of Austria is famous for its filled potato pockets. This specialty is usually accented with wonderful cheese made from fresh milk of the finest quality—a premium product of the idyllic Alps.

Rösti

SWITZERLAND

Five simple ingredients are all you need to make a hearty, golden rösti—the classic dish from Switzerland. Prepared with bacon, it makes a toothsome main course.

INGREDIENTS
(Serves 4)

- 1¾ pounds all-purpose potatoes (5 medium)
- salt and pepper
- 5 bacon strips
- 1 tablespoon butter
- 2 tablespoons vegetable oil

INGREDIENT TIPS

- If you want a softer pancake, replace half of the potatoes with well-drained sauerkraut.
- For a vegetarian dish, use a medium onion instead of bacon and add 2 tablespoons of oil.

1 Place the potatoes in a large saucepan with water to cover and bring to a boil. Reduce the heat and simmer until barely tender, about 35 minutes. Drain and let cool.

2 Peel and coarsely grate the potatoes. Sprinkle with ½ teaspoon salt and ¼ teaspoon pepper; toss well. Finely chop the bacon.

Step 2

3 In a large heavy skillet over medium heat, melt half of the butter in 1 tablespoon of the oil. Add the bacon and cook, stirring, for 3 minutes. Spoon the grated potatoes on top. Spread evenly in the pan. Press with a spatula to compact. Cook until golden brown underneath, about 10 minutes.

Step 3

4 With a spatula, loosen the cake from the pan. Invert a round platter on top. Flip carefully to remove the cake. Add the remaining 1 tablespoon oil and ½ tablespoon butter to the skillet. When the butter is melted, invert the cake into the pan; cook until golden on the bottom, about 10 minutes. Cut into wedges and serve.

Step 4

Preparation: 30 minutes
Cooking: 1 hour
Per serving: 361 cal; 6 g pro; 26 g fat; 27 g carb.

TYPICALLY SWISS

The bordering countries of Italy, France, Austria, and Germany have each influenced Switzerland's culture and cuisine. Swiss cooking tends to blend their diverse culinary traditions, creating rich variety.

COOKING TIPS

• It's easy to make rösti from potatoes that have been baked or boiled the day before. They're easier to work with if they've been well chilled.

• A cast-iron skillet is best for frying the cake.

SERVING TIPS

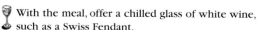

Rösti is an excellent side dish with browned chicken or veal cutlets. A green salad is the perfect complement.

With the meal, offer a chilled glass of white wine, such as a Swiss Fendant.

SOUFFLÉED POTATOES

FRANCE

INGREDIENTS
(Serves 4)

- 4 medium baking potatoes
- 3 large eggs, separated
- 3 tablespoons butter
- 1 tablespoon chopped fresh mixed herbs, such as basil, rosemary, sage, and thyme
- salt and pepper

INGREDIENT TIPS

• Choose potatoes of the same size and shape—this ensures that they'll cook in the same amount of time.

• Don't forget that the fresher the potato, the richer it will be in vitamins.

This warming, herb-scented dish—a soft, savory soufflé baked in a large potato—is a specialty of French cuisine. It tastes delicious, and it's a cinch to prepare.

1 Preheat the oven to 425°F. Scrub the potatoes well and prick with a long-pronged fork. Place on a small baking sheet and bake for 1 hour, until tender. Leave the oven on.

2 Remove the potatoes from the oven and let cool slightly. Cut a lengthwise slice from each potato, about ½ inch thick. Hold each potato in a towel in your hand and, with a fork, carefully remove the flesh.

3 In a bowl, mash the potato. Stir in the egg yolks, butter, herbs, ¾ teaspoon salt, and ¼ teaspoon pepper.

4 In a clean bowl, beat the egg whites with an electric mixer until they hold soft peaks. Gently fold the whites into the potato mixture. Spoon the filling into the potato shells.

5 Return the potatoes to the baking sheet and bake in the hot oven for 30 minutes, until golden. Serve immediately.

Step 2

Step 2

Step 4

Preparation: 30 minutes
Baking: 1½ hours.
Per serving: 258 cal; 7 g pro; 12 g fat; 30 g carb.

TYPICALLY PROVENÇAL
Since Roman times, the dry land of the South of France has produced the herbs that make up the world-famous herbes de Provence. Included in this seasoning is lavender—the small flowers with their intense yet pleasant fragrance are harvested just before they open.

COOKING TIP

Test the potatoes for doneness (during initial cooking) by inserting a thin wooden skewer or toothpick. Keep them in the oven until they're very soft, and be careful when scooping out the cooked potato—don't burn yourself. And try to keep the potato skin intact!

SERVING TIPS

Make this dish a meal with a hearty and refreshing *salade niçoise,* which features tuna and olives.

 You might offer a nice rosé wine, such as a Tavel, or a refreshing iced tea.

POTATOES AU GRATIN

FRANCE

A French gratin is any dish that's topped with cheese or a buttery bread-crumb mixture, then oven-broiled until golden and crisp. Serve it as a light main or hearty side dish.

INGREDIENTS
(Serves 4)

- 2½ pounds all-purpose potatoes
- salt and pepper
- 1 large onion
- 3 tablespoons unsalted butter, plus more for greasing the casserole
- 6 ounces Gruyère cheese, coarsely grated
- 1 cup heavy cream
- ¼ cup chopped parsley
- ¾ cup finely grated Parmesan cheese

INGREDIENT TIPS

- For variety, you can add 4 ounces of finely diced ham or ¼ cup crumbled cooked bacon to the gratin.
- Instead of Gruyère, any Swiss—or other semisoft cheese—can be used.

1 Peel the potatoes; slice ⅛ inch thick. Place in a large saucepan with water to cover and 1 teaspoon salt. Bring to a boil; cook for 2 minutes, then drain and pat dry.

2 Halve and peel the onion, then thinly slice. Melt the butter in a large skillet over medium heat until bubbly. Add the onion and cook, stirring occasionally, until golden and soft, about 15 minutes.

3 Preheat the oven to 375°F. Butter a shallow 1½-quart casserole. Spread the caramelized onions in the bottom of the dish. Top with half of the potatoes, arranging in rows. Sprinkle with ¼ teaspoon salt and ⅛ teaspoon pepper. Top with the Gruyère. Arrange the remaining potatoes on top.

4 Stir together the cream and parsley. Pour evenly over the potatoes. Sprinkle the Parmesan cheese on top. Cover the dish snugly with foil and bake for 20 minutes. Uncover; bake for 20–30 minutes more, until nicely browned. Let cool slightly and serve.

Step 1

Step 3

Step 4

Preparation: 25 minutes
Baking: 50 minutes
Per serving: 738 cal; 26 g pro; 51 g fat; 46 g carb.

TYPICALLY FRENCH

A version of this potato dish originated in Dauphiné, a French region situated between the Rhône Valley and the Italian border. Inhabitants of this area love homey gratins served hot from the oven.

COOKING TIPS

• Parboiling the potato slices insures they will be meltingly tender once the gratin is baked.

• For a lighter option, the heavy cream can be replaced with half-and-half (although heavy cream makes the dish more velvety).

SERVING TIPS

A fresh tomato salad goes well with the potatoes. Dress it with a balsamic vinaigrette.

 Offer a French red wine, such as a Beaujolais, with this meal.

DUMPLINGS—THREE WAYS

Sweet and savory fillings lend distinctive flavor to each of these dumplings, which come from three European traditions.

APRICOT BUNDLES

Preparation: 1½ hours   Cooking: 15 minutes

AUSTRIA

(SERVES 8)

- 3 small baking potatoes
- 1 egg plus 1 egg yolk
- ½ cup plus 1 tablespoon all-purpose flour
- ¼ cup farina
- 1 slice stale bread, cubed
- salt
- 16 small sugar cubes
- 8 small apricots, halved
- 1 stick (4 ounces) butter
- 3 ounces bread crumbs
- 1–2 tablespoons sugar

1 Preheat the oven to 400°F. Scrub the potatoes, pierce all over with a fork, wrap in foil, and bake for 1 hour, until tender. Peel; press through a ricer onto a clean towel. Let rest for 20 minutes. Add the egg, yolk, flour, farina, bread cubes, and ½ teaspoon salt; knead until very smooth.

2 Place a sugar cube in the center of each apricot half. With wet hands, shape equal amounts of the potato dough around each apricot half to form a ball. Simmer dumplings in a large saucepan of boiling water for 15 minutes, until they float. Remove with a slotted spoon; let stand for 5 minutes.

3 Melt the butter; mix with the bread crumbs. Roll the dumplings in the crumbs and sprinkle with the sugar.

MUSHROOM

Preparation: 1½ hours

DENMARK

(SERVES 4)

- 3 small baking potatoes
- 1 egg plus 1 egg yolk
- ½ cup plus 1 tablespoon all-purpose flour
- ¼ cup farina
- 1 slice stale bread, cubed
- salt and pepper
- ¼ teaspoon nutmeg
- 1 small onion
- 3 ounces mushrooms
- 2 bacon strips
- 1 tablespoon chopped parsley

1 Prepare the potato dough with the potatoes, egg, egg yolk, flour, farina, bread cubes, and salt as

PUFFS

Cooking: 15 minutes

directed for the Apricot Bundles, adding a pinch of pepper
and the nutmeg to the dough.

2 Peel the onion. Finely chop
the onion, mushrooms, and
bacon. In a large skillet, cook
the bacon and onion over medium heat for 10 minutes. Add
the mushrooms, ¼ teaspoon
each salt and pepper, and the
parsley; sauté for 5 minutes.

3 With wet hands, shape the
potato dough into 16 balls;
press some of the bacon mixture into the middle of each.
Simmer dumplings in a large
saucepan of boiling salted
water for 15 minutes,
until they float.

SPINACH DUMPLINGS

Preparation: 1½ hours   Cooking: 15 minutes

SWITZERLAND

(SERVES 4)
- 3 small baking potatoes
- 1 egg plus 1 egg yolk
- ½ cup plus 1 tablespoon
  all-purpose flour
- ¼ cup farina
- 1 slice stale bread, cubed
- salt and pepper
- ¼ teaspoon nutmeg
- 4 bacon strips
- 1 onion
- 4 ounces fresh spinach
- 4 ounces Emmentaler
  cheese

1 Prepare the potato dough
with the potatoes, egg, egg
yolk, flour, farina, bread cubes,
and salt as directed for the

Apricot Bundles, adding a
pinch of pepper and the nutmeg to the dough.

2 Dice the bacon. Peel and
dice the onion. Rinse, dry,
and finely chop the spinach. In
a large skillet, cook the bacon
and onion over medium heat
for 10 minutes. Add the
spinach; cook for 3 minutes.
Knead the mixture into the
dough. Finely grate the cheese.

3 With wet hands, shape
the potato dough into
16 balls; press some of the
cheese into the middle of
each. Simmer in a large saucepan of boiling salted water for
15 minutes, until they float.

TAPAS-STYLE SKILLET POTATOES

SPAIN

Simple and sensationally good, these crisp fried potatoes are perfect as a snack with beer or wine. The rich garlic mayonnaise is indispensable as an accompaniment.

INGREDIENTS
(Serves 6)

- 1½ pounds medium all-purpose potatoes

FOR THE MAYONNAISE
- 1 large egg yolk, at room temperature
- 1 tablespoon flour
- 2 tablespoons lemon juice
- 1 tablespoon plus ½ cup olive oil
- ½ teaspoon dry mustard
- 2 garlic cloves
- salt and white pepper

IN ADDITION
- ½ cup olive oil for frying

INGREDIENT TIP

If possible, use an extra-virgin olive oil with a deeper color for the mayonnaise; the flavor is more intense. For frying, any mild olive oil or vegetable oil is fine.

1 Place the unpeeled potatoes in a large saucepan with water to cover. Bring to a simmer and cook until barely fork-tender, about 30 minutes. Drain and let cool.

2 Place the egg yolk in a medium bowl; beat with a whisk until frothy. Set aside. In a small saucepan, whisk together the flour, lemon juice, and 1 tablespoon of the oil. Whisk in ½ cup water. Bring to a boil, stirring constantly. Reduce the heat and simmer for 5 minutes, stirring often.

3 Gradually beat the hot liquid into the egg yolk, adding it bit by bit. Let cool to room temperature, then beat in the remaining ½ cup oil, pouring in a fine stream until incorporated. Stir in the mustard. Peel the garlic and push through a press into the mayonnaise. Season with ½ teaspoon salt and ⅛ teaspoon white pepper.

4 Peel the potatoes; cut into ¾-inch dice. Heat the oil in a large skillet over medium-high heat. Add the potatoes; cook for 15 minutes, until golden. Drain on paper towels. Sprinkle with ½ teaspoon salt and ⅛ teaspoon pepper. Serve with mayonnaise.

Step 2

Step 4

Step 4

Preparation: 45 minutes
Cooking: 15 minutes
Per serving: 406 cal; 3 g pro;
35 g fat; 22 g carb.

TYPICALLY SPANISH

Tapas are small, tasty dishes offered in bars and restaurants all over Spain. An assortment of them makes a nice light meal. *Tapa* means "lid"—bartenders used to cover glasses of wine with small plates of savory morsels that were on the house. Today tapas are rarely free.

COOKING TIP

You can also serve these potatoes with a spicy red sauce. Fry ¼ cup diced onions in 1 tablespoon olive oil until soft. Add 2 crushed garlic cloves and a chopped jalapeño; cook 1 minute. Add a 28-ounce can crushed tomatoes. Simmer until thick; season.

SERVING TIPS

Offer the dish with olives, fried shrimp, and marinated peppers, and your tapas are complete.

A small glass of dry or semidry sherry is the customary pairing with these tidbits.

VEGETABLE TORTILLA

Spanish cuisine is famous for its versatile omelet, the tortilla. Summer squash and red bell peppers turn this luscious potato classic into a delicacy—and a treat for vegetarians.

INGREDIENTS
(Serves 4)

- 1½ pounds firm potatoes
- 1 zucchini
- 1 small red bell pepper
- 1 onion
- 1 garlic clove
- 5 tablespoons olive oil
- salt and black pepper
- ¼ cup chopped parsley
- 8 large eggs, beaten

INGREDIENT TIP

The bell peppers and the squash can be replaced with green beans, peas, carrots, or broccoli. Shrimp, ham, or chorizo would make a great addition to the vegetables.

1 Peel and thinly slice the potatoes and zucchini. Halve the bell pepper; discard the seeds and ribs. Finely dice the pepper. Peel the onion and thinly slice. Peel and finely chop the garlic.

Step 1

2 In a large nonstick skillet, heat 3 tablespoons oil over medium heat. Add the potatoes, ½ teaspoon salt, and ¼ teaspoon black pepper and cook, stirring occasionally, for 15 minutes. Transfer to a plate.

3 Add 1 tablespoon oil and the onion to the skillet and cook for 3 minutes. Stir in the garlic and cook for 1 minute. Add the bell pepper; cook for 2 minutes. Add the zucchini, ½ teaspoon salt, and ¼ teaspoon black pepper and cook, turning, for 3 minutes. Stir in the parsley and cooked potatoes.

Step 4

4 Add the remaining 1 tablespoon oil to the skillet; pour in the eggs, stirring to mix with the vegetables. Cover; cook over low heat for 8 minutes, shaking the pan. Slide the tortilla onto a platter. Invert into the skillet and cook the other side for 3 minutes, until golden. Cut the tortilla into wedges and serve.

Step 4

Preparation: 15 minutes
Cooking: 35 minutes
Per serving: 428 cal; 16 g pro;
27 g fat; 31 g carb.

TYPICALLY SPANISH

The original Spanish version of the Italian frittata, the tortilla, consists only of eggs, potatoes, and oil for frying, though onion is often added. The most important ingredient in this traditional dish is the potato, which the Spanish conquistadors brought back with them from the New World.

32 *The Mediterranean*

COOKING TIPS

• You can also remove the tortilla from the skillet with the help of a plate that's slightly larger than the pan. Simply hold the plate over the pan with pot holders and invert.

• Take care not to overcook the eggs—the dish tastes best when it's still slightly soft.

SERVING TIPS

Offer wedges of the tortilla as an appetizer, or serve with salad and bread for light dinner fare.

🍷 A cool glass of Spanish white wine—such as a Ribeiro—tastes best with this dish.

CHEESE-FILLED POTATO CROQUETTES

ITALY

Your guests will love this winning variation of Italian rice croquettes—the perfect accompaniment to a succulent entree. Here, soft melted cheese is hidden in a delicious potato dough.

INGREDIENTS
(Serves 4)

- 2 large baking potatoes
- salt and pepper
- 3 tablespoons chopped parsley
- pinch of nutmeg
- 2 large egg yolks
- 2 tablespoons flour
- 4 ounces mozzarella

IN ADDITION

- 1 large egg
- ½ cup plain dried bread crumbs
- ⅓ cup finely grated Parmesan cheese
- 3 cups canola oil, for frying

INGREDIENT TIP

For even richer flavor, fry the croquettes in fresh lard purchased from a butcher.

1 Place the unpeeled potatoes in a saucepan with water to cover. Bring to a boil; reduce the heat and simmer for 45 minutes, until tender. Let cool slightly, then peel and press through a ricer into a bowl.

2 Beat in ¾ teaspoon salt, ¼ teaspoon pepper, the parsley, and nutmeg. Stir in the egg yolks and flour.

Step 2

3 Cut the mozzarella into twenty 2-inch-long sticks. Divide the potato dough into 20 portions. With floured hands, form the dough into logs; press a piece of cheese into each and reshape to enclose the cheese. Each log should be about 2½ inches long.

4 In a bowl, whisk the whole egg. In a shallow bowl, toss together the bread crumbs and Parmesan cheese. Turn each log in the egg, then roll in the bread crumbs until well coated. Set aside on a plate.

Step 4

5 Heat the oil in a large saucepan over medium-high heat to 350°F. Add the croquettes to the oil in batches and cook for about 3 minutes, turning, until golden. Drain on paper towels and serve hot.

Step 5

Preparation: 1 hour
Cooking: 10 minutes

Per portion: 444 cal; 16 g pro; 27 g fat; 35 g carb.

TYPICALLY ROMAN

From the Roman kitchen comes lots of rich-tasting home-style food. But Italy's lively capital city does not rely on butter—cheeses, pork fat, and olive oil are often used to lend sumptuous flavor to the local fare.

COOKING TIPS

• To make your croquettes uniform in shape, roll the dough into a 1-inch-thick cylinder, then cut it into 2-inch pieces.

• Use a slotted spoon to remove the cooked croquettes from the oil.

SERVING TIPS

Enjoy this side dish with a lean steak or chop and a green salad with a light vinaigrette.

 A dry Frascati from southeast of Rome tastes great with the meal.

CRISPY HERB POTATOES

ITALY

These baked potatoes—wonderfully seasoned with Parmesan, rosemary, thyme, and garlic—will fill your kitchen with a mouthwatering aroma, luring family and friends to the table.

INGREDIENTS
(Serves 4)

- 4 large, firm potatoes
- 1 tablespoon fresh rosemary leaves, plus some sprigs for garnish
- 1½ teaspoons fresh thyme leaves
- 4 garlic cloves
- ¼ cup plain bread crumbs
- 2 ounces Parmesan cheese
- 2 tablespoons butter
- 2 tablespoons olive oil
- salt and pepper

INGREDIENT TIPS

• Freshly grated Parmesan cheese is more flavorful than packaged grated cheese.
• You can substitute ½ teaspoon *each* dried rosemary and thyme for the fresh herbs.

1 Preheat the oven to 425°F. Grease a baking sheet. Peel the potatoes and halve lengthwise. Slice the potato halves on an angle at ¼-inch intervals, without slicing all the way through (see Cooking Tip).

2 Finely chop the rosemary and thyme. Peel the garlic and finely mince. Mix the herbs and garlic with the bread crumbs; sprinkle this mixture over the potatoes. Finely grate the Parmesan and sprinkle on top of the potatoes.

3 Melt the butter in a small saucepan over low heat. Stir in the olive oil, 1 teaspoon salt, and ½ teaspoon pepper; drizzle the mixture over the potatoes with a spoon.

4 Place the potatoes in the hot oven and bake for about 30 minutes, until fork-tender, crisp, and golden brown. Transfer with a large metal spatula to a platter or plates. Garnish with rosemary and serve.

Step 1

Step 2

Step 4

Preparation: 25 minute
Baking: 30 minutes
Per serving: 333 cal; 10 g pro; 17 g fat; 37 g carb.

TYPICALLY ITALIAN
In Apulia, the region in the heel of the boot of Italy, farming is an important part of life. Often featured on the menu in this part of the country are vegetable and potato dishes. They're traditionally seasoned with olive oil, garlic, and locally grown herbs.

COOKING TIP

To ensure that the potato slices remain connected, place each potato half on the cutting board with a wooden skewer or chopstick on each side. Then slice through the potato on a diagonal—the skewer will keep the knife from going all the way through.

SERVING TIPS

With a mixed salad, this dish makes great light fare. It's also a perfect complement to broiled lamb chops.

 Offer a crisp white wine, sparkling mineral water, or water with lemon wedges.

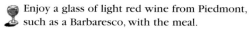

SERVING TIPS Gnocchi are also excellent topped with pesto, the Italian fresh basil sauce.

Enjoy a glass of light red wine from Piedmont, such as a Barbaresco, with the meal.

38

GNOCCHI POMODORO

A delicacy enjoyed in the beautiful Piedmont region of Italy, gnocchi with fresh tomato and sage is unbeatable. The light sauce is a perfect topping for the tender potato dumplings.

INGREDIENTS
(Serves 4)

- 4 large baking potatoes (about 2 pounds)
- 1¼ cups all-purpose flour

FOR THE SAUCE
- 2 pounds plum tomatoes
- 1 onion
- 2 garlic cloves
- 2 tablespoons butter
- ⅓ cup fresh sage leaves
- salt and pepper

IN ADDITION
- ⅔ cup freshly grated Parmesan cheese for sprinkling

INGREDIENT TIP
If you can't find fresh, juicy plum tomatoes, feel free to substitute a drained 35-ounce can of peeled tomatoes.

1 Peel and quarter the potatoes. Place in a saucepan with salted water to cover. Cook until tender, about 20 minutes. Drain; press through a ricer into a bowl. Meanwhile, peel, seed, and dice the tomatoes.

2 Peel and finely chop the onion and garlic. Melt the butter in a medium skillet over medium heat. Add the sage; cook until crisp. Transfer to a plate. Add the onion and garlic to the pan and cook, stirring often, until tender, about 5 minutes. Add the tomatoes, ½ teaspoon salt, and ¼ teaspoon pepper. Bring to a simmer; cook for 30 minutes, stirring occasionally. Keep warm.

3 Bring a pot of salted water to a boil. Add ½ teaspoon salt, ¼ teaspoon pepper, and the flour to the potatoes. Stir until blended. Divide the dough into quarters. On a floured board with floured hands, shape each into a 16-inch-long rope; cut into ½-inch pieces. Press each piece with a flour-dipped fork to make a striped pattern.

4 Add the gnocchi to the boiling water and let cook until they float, about 5 minutes. Drain, transfer to a plate, and top with the sauce, sage leaves, and Parmesan.

Step 2

Step 3

Step 4

Preparation: 1 hour
Cooking: 5 minutes
Per serving: 483 cal; 17 g pro; 11 g fat; 81 g carb.

TYPICALLY PIEDMONTESE
Little pasta dumplings like these are much loved in Northern Italy. Potato gnocchi are particular favorites in Piedmont, where they are enjoyed in various ways. Also popular are semolina and cornmeal gnocchi.

ℒEMON-GARLIC POTATOES

GREECE

This aromatic side dish from Greece features small new potatoes browned in olive oil and simmered in a flavorful broth with lemon, garlic, rosemary, and thyme.

INGREDIENTS
(Serves 4)

- 5 garlic cloves
- ¼ cup olive oil
- 1⅔ pounds small red potatoes
- 1 cup chicken broth
- salt and pepper
- 1 lemon
- 3 fresh thyme sprigs
- 1 fresh rosemary sprig

IN ADDITION
- thyme and rosemary sprigs for garnish

INGREDIENT TIPS

• Try to find uniform, small potatoes to ensure that they cook evenly.
• The fresh herbs can be replaced with ½ teaspoon *each* of dried rosemary and thyme. Fresh parsley and mint are also good options.

1 Peel the garlic and slice as thinly as possible. Warm the oil in a large cast-iron skillet over low heat. Add the garlic and cook gently, stirring often, until fragrant and lightly golden, about 2 minutes. Using a slotted spoon, transfer the garlic to a plate.

2 Add the potatoes to the pan, turning to coat in the oil. Cook over medium heat, shaking the pan, until the potatoes are golden, about 10 minutes. Pour in the broth and add ¼ teaspoon *each* salt and pepper. Cover the pan and simmer until the potatoes are tender, about 25 minutes.

3 Finely grate the peel from the lemon and squeeze the juice. Finely chop the thyme and rosemary. Add the lemon juice, lemon peel, thyme, and rosemary to the potatoes.

4 Cook the potatoes, uncovered, over medium-high heat until only a few tablespoons of liquid remain, about 5 minutes. Stir in the garlic. Transfer to a platter and garnish with thyme and rosemary sprigs.

Step 1

Step 3

Step 3

Preparation: 10 minutes
Cooking: 45 minutes
Per serving: 290 cal; 4 g pro;
14 g fat; 37 g carb.

TYPICALLY GREEK
Potatoes have been adored by Greeks for centuries. In the rugged Peloponnesian peninsula of southern Greece, potatoes thrive alongside grains, olives, fruits, and vegetables.

COOKING TIP

Greek-style mashed potatoes have a similar flavor to the whole ones in this recipe. To make them, cook 1 pound potatoes, then drain, peel, and mash. Sauté 3 crushed garlic cloves in $\frac{1}{3}$ cup olive oil. Stir into the potatoes with $\frac{1}{3}$–$\frac{1}{2}$ cup chicken broth. Add salt, pepper, and lemon juice to taste.

SERVING TIPS

For a simple, savory light bite, serve the potatoes with roasted red bell peppers and feta cheese.

 A Greek red wine goes perfectly with this meal. Try a dry fruity Demestica.

SERVING TIPS Offer the vegetable medley as an appetizer along with goat cheese, olives, and pita.

Raki, an anise-flavored spirit, and ayran, a cool yogurt drink, are ideal beverages with this dish.

POTATO-EGGPLANT MEDLEY

TURKEY

INGREDIENTS
(Serves 4)

- 1 eggplant (1-1½ pounds)
- 2 mild frying chiles
- 5 tablespoons olive oil
- 1 pound all-purpose potatoes
- ½ teaspoon paprika

FOR THE YOGURT SAUCE
- ¼ cup parsley leaves
- ¼ cup mint leaves
- 1 garlic clove
- 1 cup plain yogurt
- salt and black pepper

INGREDIENT TIP
Creamy whole-milk yogurt lends distinctive richness to Turkish cuisine. You can use low-fat yogurt—just be sure it's well chilled.

Sautéed potatoes and eggplant with a hint of lively chile is one of the best Turkish vegetable combinations. Serve it with the cool herbed yogurt sauce as an appetizer or a side dish.

1 Cut the eggplant into ¾-inch pieces. Thinly slice the chiles into rings. Heat 3 tablespoons of the oil in a large nonstick skillet over medium-high heat. Add the eggplant and cook for 8 minutes, stirring. Add the chiles and cook until the eggplant and chiles are tender, about 5 minutes. Transfer to a plate.

2 Peel and dice the potatoes into ¾-inch pieces. Heat the remaining 2 tablespoons oil in the pan. Add the potatoes and cook, turning occasionally, until tender and golden, about 20 minutes.

3 Meanwhile, finely chop the parsley, mint, and garlic. Place in a bowl and add the yogurt; stir until blended. Season to taste with salt and black pepper. Refrigerate until ready to serve.

4 Return the eggplant and chile to the pan with the potatoes. Sprinkle with the paprika, ¾ teaspoon salt, and ¼ teaspoon black pepper. Stir until heated through, then transfer the mixture to a serving platter. Serve the yogurt sauce on the side.

Step 2

Step 3

Step 4

Preparation: 15 minutes
Cooking: 40 minutes
Per serving: 334 cal; 7 g pro;
21 g fat; 31 g carb.

TYPICALLY TURKISH
Ever since the days when the ancestors of the Turkish people roamed the land as nomads, yogurt has been an integral part of their diet. The Turks often make the fresh sour-milk product at home, sometimes with sheep's milk but also with goat or cow's milk.

VEGETABLE KABOBS

Surprise your guests with this unusual vegetarian appetizer or light main dish—potatoes and colorful vegetables basted with seasoned olive oil and grilled on skewers.

INGREDIENTS
(Serves 4)

- 1 pound oval white potatoes
- 2 fresh thyme sprigs plus additional for garnish
- 6 tablespoons olive oil
- salt and black pepper
- ½ teaspoon ground cumin
- ¼ teaspoon ground cardamom
- ¼ teaspoon chili powder
- ⅛ teaspoon cinnamon
- 1 mild onion
- 2 small zucchini
- 1 red bell pepper
- 8 fresh bay leaves

INGREDIENT TIPS

- Sweet onions—such as Vidalia, Texas Sweets, or Walla Walla—are best for this dish.
- If you can't find fresh bay leaves, omit them (don't use the dried variety here).

1 Rinse, scrub, and peel the potatoes. Cut into ½-inch slices. Simmer in a saucepan of salted water until softened but not tender, about 5 minutes. Drain.

2 Remove the thyme leaves from 2 of the sprigs and place in a large bowl. Add the oil, ½ teaspoon salt, ¼ teaspoon black pepper, the cumin, cardamom, chili powder, and cinnamon. Mix well. Add the potatoes.

3 Peel the onion and cut in half lengthwise. Carefully separate its layers and place in the bowl with the potatoes. Cut the zucchini into ½-inch slices and add to the potatoes. Seed and devein the bell pepper and cut into pieces similar in size to the potatoes. Add to the potatoes. Toss the vegetables to coat with the herb mixture.

4 Thread the vegetables onto 4 wooden skewers, alternating the kinds of vegetables and interspersing halves of bay leaves between them. Reserve the remaining herb mixture.

5 Grill the kabobs on all sides until golden, about 10 minutes, basting with the herb mixture. Garnish with thyme sprigs.

Step 3

Step 4

Step 5

Preparation: 30 minutes
Cooking: 10 minutes
Per serving: 298 cal; 4 g pro; 21 g fat; 27 g carb.

TYPICALLY ISRAELI

Grilled skewers of all kinds are very popular restaurant and street fare throughout Israel. Ideal complements to many meals, they're a must at barbecues, where vegetarian skewers are served alongside the meat course.

COOKING TIPS

• The potatoes must be cooked before grilling or they'll be too hard. However, it's important not to precook them for too long. Slices that are too soft will be difficult to skewer.

• The vegetables can be tossed with the herb mixture up to 2 hours before cooking.

SERVING TIPS

The perfect accompaniment is a tomato dipping sauce seasoned with garlic and parsley.

🧂 Drink mineral water with fresh lemon or beer with this meal.

GINGER-CURRY POTATOES

INDIA

A blend of typical Indian spices enhances this luscious potato dish. Fresh tomatoes add color, and black sesame seeds are a wonderfully aromatic finishing touch.

INGREDIENTS
(Serves 4)

- 1½ pounds all-purpose potatoes
- 2 tablespoons vegetable oil
- 3 scallions
- 2 garlic cloves
- 1-inch piece fresh ginger
- 1 jalapeño chile
- 2 tomatoes
- 1-2 tablespoons curry powder
- 1 cup plain yogurt
- 1 tablespoon all-purpose flour
- 1-2 tablespoons lemon juice
- salt and pepper
- 1 tablespoon black sesame seeds

INGREDIENT TIP

Black sesame seeds are available at Asian and Middle Eastern markets. White sesame seeds, roasted until fragrant, can be used instead.

1 Rinse, scrub, and peel the potatoes; cut into ¾-inch pieces. Cook in a saucepan of boiling salted water just until fork-tender, about 5 minutes. Drain, rinse with cold water, and pat dry. Heat the oil in a large skillet and fry the potatoes over medium-high heat, stirring often, until golden brown, 10–12 minutes.

Step 2

2 While the potatoes cook, trim off the tough green portion of the scallions and thinly slice the remainder, reserving 1 tablespoon of the tender green portion for garnish. Peel and finely chop the garlic and ginger. Seed, devein, and finely chop the jalapeño. Seed and cube the tomatoes.

Step 2

3 Add the curry powder to the potatoes and fry over low heat for 2 minutes, stirring constantly. Add the scallions, garlic, ginger, and jalapeño and cook, stirring, for 5 minutes.

4 Mix the yogurt with the flour and stir into the potato mixture. Cook over low heat for 2–3 minutes, until heated through. Stir in lemon juice to taste and ¼ teaspoon *each* salt and pepper. Sprinkle with the reserved scallion and the sesame seeds.

Step 4

Preparation: 45 minutes
Cooking: 30 minutes

Per serving: 248 cal; 7 g pro; 9 g fat; 36 g carb.

TYPICALLY INDIAN

For religious reasons, many people in India are vegetarians. No wonder the Indian vegetarian kitchen is so diverse and flavorful! The spices here make the dish come alive.

COOKING TIP

Indians most often fry with ghee, a type of clarified butter, instead of oil. Without the milk solids of regular butter, ghee can be used for frying at high temperatures. Look for ghee in Indian markets. If you can't find it, simply use vegetable oil.

SERVING TIPS

Grilled fish or chicken tastes great with this dish. Serve with flat bread, such as chapatis, nan, or pita.

 Offer a cool lassi (a yogurt drink) or hot spice tea as a beverage.

SERVING TIPS Offer a tangy tomato or fruity mango chutney with this dish.

 Indian spice tea, laced with cardamom, cinnamon, and cloves, is an ideal beverage here.

INDIAN-SPICED POTATO ROLLS

INDIA

Here's a delicious snack or unusual side dish. A seasoned potato puree is layered onto and rolled up in dough, cut into slices, and fried until golden brown.

INGREDIENTS
(Serves 4)

- 1½ pounds baking potatoes
- 6 tablespoons unsweetened grated coconut
- 2 tablespoons sesame seeds
- 1 large jalapeño chile
- 2-inch piece fresh ginger
- 2 teaspoons curry powder
- salt
- 2 packages (8 ounces *each*) refrigerated crescent-roll dough

IN ADDITION
- 8 cups vegetable oil for frying

INGREDIENT TIP

Toasting the sesame seeds adds crunch and flavor to the potato filling. To save a little time, you can substitute raw black sesame seeds.

1 Place the potatoes in a large saucepan with salted water to cover. Bring to a boil, reduce the heat, and simmer, partially covered, until the potatoes are fork-tender, about 45 minutes. Drain, peel, and press the potatoes through a ricer into a large bowl.

2 In a small dry skillet, roast the coconut and sesame seeds over medium heat, stirring often, until toasted, about 3 minutes. Trim and halve the chile, remove the seeds and veins, then finely chop. Peel and grate the ginger; add to the potatoes along with the coconut, sesame seeds, chile, curry powder, and ½ teaspoon salt.

3 On a floured board, roll out 1 package of dough to a 12 x 9-inch rectangle. Spread half of the potato mixture on top. Starting from a longer side, roll up the dough jelly-roll fashion. Trim, then cut into 10 slices. Repeat with the remaining dough and filling.

4 Heat the oil in a large pot to 350°F. Add the potato rolls in batches. Cook, turning, until golden and crisp, about 2 minutes. Drain on paper towels and serve warm.

Step 1

Step 3

Step 3

Preparation: 25 minutes
Cooking: 1 hour
Per serving: 707 cal; 12 g pro; 40 g fat; 79 g carb.

TYPICALLY BENGALI

Calcutta, in the Indian state of West Bengal, was founded by the British in the late 17th century and was later the capital of British India. The colonizers brought with them their beloved potato, which soon became a valued source of nutrition for Indians as well.

TWICE-BAKED POTATOES—THREE WAYS

Traditionally served as a side dish with steak, a baked potato stuffed with cheese, beans, or vegetables can be a meal in itself.

BASIC BAKED POTATO

The preparation of the potatoes will always be the same.
Make the filling while they are baking in the oven.

1 Preheat the oven to 425°F. Rinse and scrub 4 medium baking potatoes. Pat dry and pierce with a fork.

2 Wrap each potato in foil with the dull side of the foil facing out. Place the potatoes on a baking sheet.

3 Bake until the potatoes are tender when pierced with a fork, about 1 hour.

ZESTY TOMATO AND MOZZARELLA

Preparation: 25 minutes   Baking: 1 hour

ITALY

(SERVES 4)
- Basic Baked Potato
- 1 tablespoon pine nuts
- 2 small tomatoes
- 1 garlic clove, crushed
- ¼ cup shredded mozzarella
- ¼ cup *each* chopped basil and parsley leaves
- salt and pepper

4 Toast the pine nuts in a dry skillet over medium heat. Chop and place in a bowl.

5 Seed and dice the tomatoes. Add the tomatoes, garlic, cheese, herbs, and ½ teaspoon *each* salt and pepper to the pine nuts; mix well.

6 Cut an X in the potatoes; squeeze open. Top each with cheese mixture, and bake for 3 minutes.

CREAMY BROCCOLI AND CHEESE

Preparation: 25 minutes   Baking: 1 hour

USA

(SERVES 4)
- Basic Baked Potato
- 3 cups broccoli florets
- ⅔ cup sour cream
- 2 tablespoons chopped parsley
- salt and pepper
- 1 cup grated cheddar or Gouda

4 In a medium sauce-pan of boiling salted water, cook the broccoli just until tender, about 3 minutes. Drain.

5 In a large bowl, combine the sour cream, the parsley, and ½ teaspoon *each* salt and pepper. Add the broccoli; toss to coat.

6 Cut an X in the potatoes and squeeze open. Divide half the cheese among the potatoes. Add the broccoli mixture and sprinkle with the remaining cheese. Bake for 5 minutes.

SPICY CHILE 'N BEAN

Preparation: 25 minutes   Baking: 1 hour

MEXICO

(SERVES 4)
- Basic Baked Potato
- 1 onion
- 1 garlic clove
- 1 jalapeño chile
- 2 tablespoons corn oil
- 1 can (19 ounces) kidney beans
- ½ cup salsa
- salt and pepper
- 1 small avocado
- 2 teaspoons lemon juice

4 Peel and chop the onion and garlic. Seed, devein, and chop the jalapeño. Heat the oil in a large nonstick skillet over medium heat. Sauté the onion, garlic, and jalapeño for 2 minutes.

5 Rinse and drain the beans and add to the onion mixture. Stir in the salsa and ½ teaspoon *each* salt and pepper. Cook over low heat for 10 minutes.

6 Halve, pit, peel, and cube the avocado. Place in a bowl and toss with the lemon juice.

7 Cut an X in the potatoes and squeeze open. Top with the bean mixture and the avocado.

AUSSIE BURGERS

AUSTRALIA

INGREDIENTS
(Serves 4)

- 1½ pounds medium baking potatoes
- 2 ounces cooked ham
- 2 ounces Emmentaler cheese
- 1 egg, beaten
- 2 tablespoons chopped parsley
- salt and pepper
- ¼ cup bread crumbs
- 4 hamburger buns
- 1 bunch of watercress
- ½ cup sour cream or crème fraîche
- 3 tablespoons chili sauce
- vegetable oil for frying

INGREDIENT TIP

The watercress can be replaced with any bitter green, such as arugula; or try a tender, sweet lettuce, such as Boston or Bibb.

Here's a delicious variation of the common hamburger. Mashed potatoes are mixed with ham and cheese, shaped into patties, and served on a bun with watercress and chili sauce.

1 Preheat the oven to 450°F. Bake the potatoes until fork-tender, about 50 minutes. Cool slightly. With a spoon, scoop the flesh into a bowl; mash coarsely.

Step 1

2 Cube the ham and cheese and add to the potatoes. Add the egg, parsley, and ½ teaspoon *each* salt and pepper. Mix well.

3 Divide the potato mixture into 4 portions and, with floured hands, shape each into a patty. Coat the patties with the bread crumbs and place on a plate. Refrigerate the patties until firm, about 1 hour.

Step 2

4 Heat the oil in a nonstick skillet over medium heat and fry the burgers for 6–7 minutes on each side, until golden.

5 Split and toast the buns. Rinse, drain, and dry the watercress. In a small bowl, mix the sour cream with the chili sauce. Spread the sauce on the bottom halves of the buns, and top with the watercress and the burgers. Spread the remaining sauce on the burgers and cover with the bun tops.

Step 3

Preparation: 20 minutes
Chilling: 1 hour
Cooking: 1 hour
Per serving: 526 cal; 19 g pro; 22 g fat; 64 g carb.

TYPICALLY AUSTRALIAN
In the days of colonization, British settlers in Australia brought with them many new foods. Among them was spicy, crisp watercress. Efficient irrigation systems keep the crop well supplied with clear, fresh water.

COOKING TIP

Vary the flavor of the burgers by using different cheeses. Monterey Jack with jalapeños, Vermont cheddar with sage, smoked Gouda, or tangy Cheshire are some of the more unusual possibilities to complement the ham and potato base.

SERVING TIPS

Let your guests top their burgers with ready-made sauces, such as ketchup, mayonnaise, and Tabasco.

The Australians drink ice-cold beer or lemonade with this type of food.

ℬAKED POTATO FANS

USA

Here, three kinds of fresh herb combinations add wonderful flavor—as well as decorative flair—to these golden-brown baked potatoes. It's a simple dish that's perfect for entertaining.

INGREDIENTS
(Serves 4)

- 12 small white potatoes
- salt and pepper
- 3 tablespoons olive oil plus additional to grease the roasting pan
- 2 tablespoons butter
- 2 tablespoons chopped fresh parsley
- 1 tablespoon *each* chopped fresh basil and oregano
- 1 teaspoon paprika
- 1 small red chile, minced
- 1 tablespoon chopped cilantro
- 2 garlic cloves
- ½ lemon
- 2 teaspoons chopped fresh rosemary

INGREDIENT TIP

Instead of white potatoes you can use other varieties such as creamy red-skinned or buttery Yukon gold.

1 Rinse, scrub, and dry the potatoes. Cut off a thin slice from one of the longer sides so that the potatoes will lie flat.

2 Slice the potatoes crosswise at ¼-inch intervals but make sure not to go all the way through. Fan them and sprinkle with salt and pepper. Preheat the oven to 400°F. Grease a roasting pan with oil.

Step 1

3 In a small saucepan, melt the butter and add the parsley, basil, and oregano. Brush the mixture over 4 potatoes.

4 In a small bowl, mix 2 tablespoons oil with the paprika; brush over 4 potatoes. Sprinkle the chile and coriander on top.

Step 4

5 Peel and finely chop the garlic and place in a small bowl. Grate the peel from the lemon half and add to the garlic. Add the rosemary. Squeeze the lemon juice into a small bowl and add the remaining 1 table-spoon oil; drizzle over the remaining 4 potatoes. Sprinkle the garlic mixture on top.

Step 5

6 Place all the potatoes cut side up in the prepared roasting pan. Bake until tender and golden brown, about 50 minutes.

Preparation: 40 minutes
Cooking: 50 minutes
Per serving: 279 cal; 4 g pro; 16 g fat; 31 g carb.

TYPICALLY IDAHO

The potato growers of several states keep America well-supplied with spuds, but Idaho is foremost among them. Consequently, many of the country's best potato recipes come from this state. Fanciful variations of baked potatoes are particularly popular.

COOKING TIP

These potatoes make a nice accompaniment to roasted meats and chicken. You can bake them in the same pan as the main course. Add them for the last 50 minutes of cooking time, or allow about 10 extra minutes if the roasting temperature is lower than 400°F.

SERVING TIPS

This side dish is perfect with a tangy salad of tomatoes, corn, bell peppers, chiles, and kidney beans.

Set a pitcher of cold sparkling cider or beer on the table to enjoy with this dish.

JALAPEÑO POTATOES

INGREDIENTS
(Serves 4)

- 1½ pounds all-purpose potatoes
- 3 tablespoons vegetable oil
- 1 red bell pepper
- 1 green bell pepper
- 1 jalapeño chile
- 1 medium red onion
- 3 small tomatoes
- salt and black pepper

IN ADDITION

- cilantro leaves
- lime or lemon wedges

INGREDIENT TIP

Fresh cilantro is what gives this dish its characteristically Mexican flavor. If this pungent herb doesn't suit your taste, you can use parsley instead.

Enjoy your potatoes the Mexican way—jazzed up with bell peppers, jalapeño chiles, and fresh tomatoes. A splash of lime juice adds zest to this colorful side dish.

1 Peel the potatoes and cut them into ½-inch slices. Heat the oil in a large, preferably cast-iron skillet. Add the potatoes and cook at medium heat, turning occasionally, until lightly browned, about 20 minutes.

2 Meanwhile, seed and devein the bell peppers and chile. Finely dice the bell peppers and mince the chile. Peel and finely chop the onion.

3 Add the bell peppers, chile, and onion to the potatoes and reduce the heat to medium-low. Cook the mixture for about 10 minutes, stirring carefully, until the potatoes are tender and golden brown.

4 Blanch, peel, stem, and crush the tomatoes. You should have about 1 cup of puree. Add the puree, ½ teaspoon salt, and ¼ teaspoon black pepper to the potatoes and simmer for 5 minutes. Garnish with cilantro leaves and lime or lemon wedges before serving.

Step 1

Step 2

Step 4

Preparation: 20 minutes
Cooking: 35 minutes
Per serving: 236 cal; 4 g pro; 11 g fat; 33 g carb.

TYPICALLY MEXICAN

Peppers and chiles of all kinds add vibrant color to the Mexican marketplace. The land of the Aztec has more than 100 indigenous varieties to offer, ranging from very mild and sweet to fiery hot.

COOKING TIP

The dish will work best if you use a pan that's large enough to give all of the potato slices good contact with the heat. Add oil even when using a nonstick pan—otherwise the potatoes won't get crisp.

SERVING TIPS

These are an ideal accompaniment to fried chicken or chorizo—the pork sausage that's popular in Mexico.

Tequila is a great aperitif. Red wine or beer is best with the meal.

ANDEAN POTATO CAKES

The people of Ecuador love their "llapingachos"—cheesy patties made with savory mashed potatoes and onions. Eat as a snack, an appetizer, or a light main course.

INGREDIENTS
(Serves 4)

- 1¾ pounds baking potatoes
- 2 onions
- 1½ tablespoons butter
- 1 large egg
- salt and pepper
- 4 ounces cheddar or Gouda cheese

IN ADDITION

- ⅓ cup all-purpose flour for forming the pancakes
- ¼ cup oil for frying
- pinch of turmeric

INGREDIENT TIP

Turmeric gives the pancakes a wonderful golden color. In Ecuador, cooks often use annatto—reddish seeds from the annatto tree—to lend dishes a similarly bright hue.

1 Scrub the potatoes. Bring a pot of salted water to a boil over high heat. Add the potatoes and cook for 20 minutes.

2 Meanwhile, peel and finely dice the onions. Melt the butter in a small saucepan over medium heat. Add the onions and sauté for 3 minutes, until tender.

Step 2

3 Drain, cool, and peel the potatoes. Pass the potatoes through a ricer into a large bowl or mash them while still warm. Add the onions, egg, ¾ teaspoon salt, and ½ teaspoon pepper. Mix well. Refrigerate for 1 hour.

Step 4

4 Cut the cheese into twelve ½-inch slices. Divide the potato mixture into 12 pieces. Form thick pancakes with floured hands. Put a piece of cheese in the middle of each one, patting the potato around the cheese. Flour the pancakes lightly.

5 Heat the oil in a 10-inch skillet; stir in the turmeric. Fry the potato pancakes for about 3–4 minutes per side, until golden and crisp. Remove with a slotted spoon and drain on paper towels before serving.

Step 5

Preparation: 30 minutes
Chilling: 1 hour
Cooking: 30 minutes
Per serving: 489 cal; 14 g pro; 26 g fat; 52 g carb.

TYPICALLY ECUADORIAN

These potato pancakes and other delectable snack foods are particularly popular in the northern Andes and the capital city of Quito, where they're sold at markets, on buses and trains, and even by the roadside.

COOKING TIP

A slightly spicy, creamy peanut sauce makes a perfect topping: In a small bowl, combine ⅓ cup smooth peanut butter, 1 minced garlic clove, ¼ teaspoon crushed red pepper, ¼ teaspoon *each* salt and black pepper, and 4 tablespoons milk. Stir until smooth and serve with the pancakes.

SERVING TIPS

A salad of sliced avocado, tomato, and lettuce is a light and refreshing complement to this dish.

 Offer iced tropical fruit juices, such as mango, guava, and passion fruit.

KITCHEN GLOSSARY

Here's an A to Z guide to some of the ingredients, cooking techniques, and kitchen equipment that are called for in this book.

CROQUETTES

These rounds of cooked meat or vegetable mixture are covered in bread crumbs and deep-fried.

FIVE-SPICE POWDER

A Chinese spice concoction made with cloves, cinnamon, pepper, fennel, and star anise.

GARAM MASALA

A blend of dry-roasted ground spices often used in Indian recipes. Ingredients vary but often include cinnamon, chiles, cloves, coriander, cumin, cardamom, fennel, mace, nutmeg, and pepper. It's available at Indian markets and gourmet food stores. In cooking, garam masala is usually added toward the end or sprinkled on just before serving.

GARLIC MAYONNAISE

Called "aïoli" in France, and popular in the Mediterranean, it often accompanies potatoes.

GNOCCHI

A specialty of Italy, these small potato dumplings are often served with a tomato or cream sauce.

GRATIN

A dish that's covered with cheese or bread crumbs, then baked or broiled in the oven until browned and bubbling.

LARD

Pork fat is melted down to make this fine white cooking fat, which allows food to cook at a very high heat and imparts a rich flavor.

MASHED POTATOES

Comfort food made from baking potatoes that are cooked and pressed in a ricer or mashed with a masher or fork. They're often mixed with cream or milk and butter.

TIPS FOR POTATOES

In the 16th century, the Spanish conquistadors brought the potato to Europe from South America. Later, European settlers brought the potato to America, where it is now consumed more than any other vegetable.

Buying

Look for firm, blemish-free potatoes with no greenish tinge on the skin. Caused by exposure to light and either too warm or too cold temperatures, the green indicates the presence of a potentially harmful toxin that can only be removed by peeling.

Storing

Keep potatoes in a cool, dark, dry place; a basement is perfect. If you lack proper storage facilities, buy only those you plan to use right away. Remove them from plastic bags and store them loosely. Don't refrigerate them.

Preparation

Potatoes shouldn't be eaten raw—the human body can't process the starch. Retain as much as you can of the peel, which contains many of the vegetable's valuable nutrients, but always thoroughly remove green spots. If you're boiling the potatoes, sprinkle a little salt into the water.

Nutritional value

So much for the myth that potatoes are fattening—they're actually fat-free and extremely low in calories (a six-ounce potato yields only about 120 calories). The vegetable is high in fiber and a great source of vitamins C and B-6, niacin, thiamin, potassium, and other important minerals.

Different Types of Potatoes

Cooking properties and harvest time are some of the criteria used when categorizing potatoes into different types.

All-purpose potatoes
Also known as boiling potatoes, these firm, waxy, lower-starch potatoes keep their integrity during cooking. They're particularly well suited to boiling and frying, and make ideal additions to soups and salads.

Baking potatoes
Also called russet, these have more starch than all-purpose potatoes and fall apart easily when cooked. They're great for baking, mashing, frying, and different kinds of dumplings.

Yellow potatoes
Also called Yukon Gold, these buttery-yellow potatoes have a smooth texture that's perfect for mashing. They're also good boiled or fried.

New potatoes
Simply young potatoes of any variety. Available from spring to early summer, they're tender and should be used right away.

Pan-Fried Potatoes
These will turn out best with firm potatoes. If you can, use a nonstick pan—but add a good amount of cooking fat so that the potatoes turn out nice and crisp. They can be jazzed up Mexican-style with hot chiles, or you can serve them with garlic mayonnaise.

Potato Pancakes
For these, raw potatoes are grated, mixed with egg, and formed into patties, then fried in hot oil until golden brown and slightly crunchy on the outside. Variations are popular all over the world, from Northern Europe to Latin America.

Rösti
Boiled potatoes that are grated, formed into a large pancake, and pan-fried. *Rösti* means "crisp and golden" in Switzerland, which is where this dish originated.

Spanish Tortilla
An omelet—made with potatoes and sometimes other vegetables—in which the ingredients are mixed with (rather than folded into) the eggs. Pan-cooked until golden and firm, it forms a thick cake.

Twice-Baked Potatoes
After large baking potatoes are baked through once, the white middle is scooped out into a bowl to be mixed with additional ingredients, such as cheeses and fresh herbs. Then the savory mixture is stuffed back into the potato skin and oven-baked a second time.

Cooking Utensils
Certain utensils are extremely helpful when cooking potatoes.

Ricer
This operates like a large garlic press. It pushes food through tiny holes to produce bits that resemble grains of rice. The ricer is ideal for making potato puree.

Masher
With this hand-held tool, you can crush boiled potatoes in the pot to make mashed potatoes.

Grater
Using a box grater, you can grate raw potatoes either finely or coarsely. This comes in handy when making potato cakes.

Peeler
Use a peeler to remove potato skins as well as brown spots and imperfections.

ℳENU SUGGESTIONS

The potato recipes in this book are either appetizers, side dishes, light main courses, or desserts. We therefore suggest two fitting companions for each recipe.

ENGLAND

PARSLIED POTATOES P. 6
*Lamb Chops with Mustard
Strawberry Butter Cake*

— ◆ —

IRELAND

COLCANNON P. 8
*Smoked Salmon
Heavenly Chocolate Trifle*

— ◆ —

SWEDEN

SALMON-POTATO SALAD P. 10
*Meatballs
Waffles with Fruit*

— ◆ —

DENMARK

POTATO CANAPÉS P. 12
*Salmon Steaks with
Red Cabbage
Cheesecake with Berries*

— ◆ —

GERMANY

CRISP POTATO PANCAKES P. 14
*Lentil Stew
Rhubarb-Strawberry Treat*

— ◆ —

SUGARED POTATO DUMPLINGS P. 16
*Beet Salad
Pork with Onions
and Sauerkraut*

— ◆ —

POLAND

POTATO-STUFFED CABBAGE P. 18
*Roast Beef
Poppy Seed Cake*

— ◆ —

AUSTRIA

HERBED POTATO POCKETS P. 20
*Country Pâté
Plum-Apricot Compote*

— ◆ —

SWITZERLAND

RÖSTI P. 22
*Veal Scallops in
Raspberry-Cream Sauce
Chocolate Pralines*

— ◆ —

FRANCE

SOUFFLÉED POTATOES P. 24
*Pike Fillets with
White Wine Sauce
Fruit and Cheese*

— ◆ —

POTATOES AU GRATIN P. 26
*Chicken à la Provençale
Pears Belle Hélène*

— ◆ —

SPAIN

TAPAS-STYLE SKILLET POTATOES P. 30
*Andalusian Chicken
with Tarragon
Chilled Melon Soup*

— ◆ —

VEGETABLE TORTILLA
P. 32
Gazpacho
Crema Catalana
— ❖ —

ITALY

CHEESE-FILLED POTATO CROQUETTES
P. 34
Roasted Leg of Lamb
Tempting Tiramisu
— ❖ —

CRISPY HERB POTATOES
P. 36
Veal Saltimbocca
Lemon-Lime Tart
— ❖ —

GNOCCHI POMODORO
P. 38
Insalata Caprese
Stuffed Peaches
— ❖ —

GREECE

LEMON-GARLIC POTATOES
P. 40
Herb-Grilled Fish
Figs in Brandy
— ❖ —

TURKEY

POTATO-EGGPLANT MEDLEY
P. 42
Fragrant Chicken Pilaf
Watermelon with
Honey Cream
— ❖ —

ISRAEL

VEGETABLE KABOBS
P. 44
Fava Bean Hummus with
Flat Bread
Orange Ice cream
— ❖ —

INDIA

GINGER-CURRY POTATOES
P. 46
Spice-Marinated
Grilled Chicken
Fragrant Mango Delight
— ❖ —

INDIAN-SPICED POTATO ROLLS
P. 48
Fruited Chicken Curry
with Toasted Coconut
Lemon Ice Cream
— ❖ —

AUSTRALIA

AUSSIE BURGERS
P. 52
Avocado-Orange Salad with
Honey-Mustard Vinaigrette
Cherry Pavlova
— ❖ —

USA

BAKED POTATO FANS
P. 54
T-bone Steak
Peach-Blueberry Cobbler
— ❖ —

MEXICO

JALAPEÑO POTATOES WITH PEPPERS   P. 56
Traditional Beef Fajitas
Tequila-Splashed Pineapple
and Banana
— ❖ —

ECUADOR

ANDEAN POTATO CAKES
P. 58
Pork with
Black Beans and Rice
Pumpkin Cake with
Caramel Sauce
— ❖ —

RECIPE INDEX

Photo Credits

Book cover and recipe photos:
©International Masters Publishers AB
Eising Food Photography, Dorothee Gödert, Peter Rees, Manuel Schnell
Agency Photos:
Introduction: Bavaria:Theissen, pages 4, 5, upper middle.
The Image Bank: Dennis, pages 4, 5, lower middle.
Helga Lade:Thompson, page 4, upper right.
Tony Stone: Brown, page 5, upper left; Allison, page 4, lower left.
Photos for the "Typically" sections: Agrar Service: Cattlin, page 52.
AKG: page 32. Bavaria:Adam, page 21; Bav, page 49; Images, page 46.
Focus: Mayr, page 18; Schwarzbach, page 30.
Fotex:Arndt, page 13; Rose, page 16. IFA:Aberham, page 43; Diaf, page 26;
Heinzhoch, page 44; Nägele, page 24; Rölle, page 58.
Image Bank: Melford, page 54; Dennis page 56.
Helga Lade: Binder, page 14; Else, page 22. Look:Acquadro, page 10.
Schapowalow:Atlantide, pages 36, 38; Fahn, page 34.
Silvestris: Rainer, page 40; Schneider and Will, page 8.